JAZZ, BLUES, & LATIN HITS
Playalong *for* Flute

Amsco Publications
A Part of **The Music Sales Group**
New York/Nashville/Los Angeles/London/Paris/Sydney/Copenhagen/Berlin/Tokyo/Madrid

Cover photography: George Taylor
Project editor: Heather Ramage

Order No. AM 988581
ISBN-10: 0.8256.3523.3
ISBN-13: 978.0.8256.3523.6

Exclusive Distributors:
Music Sales Corporation
257 Park Avenue South, New York, NY 10010 USA
Music Sales Limited
14-15 Berners Street, London W1T 3LJ England
Music Sales Pty. Limited
120 Rothschild Street, Rosebery, Sydney, NSW 2018, Australia

Printed in the United States of America

Fingering Guide

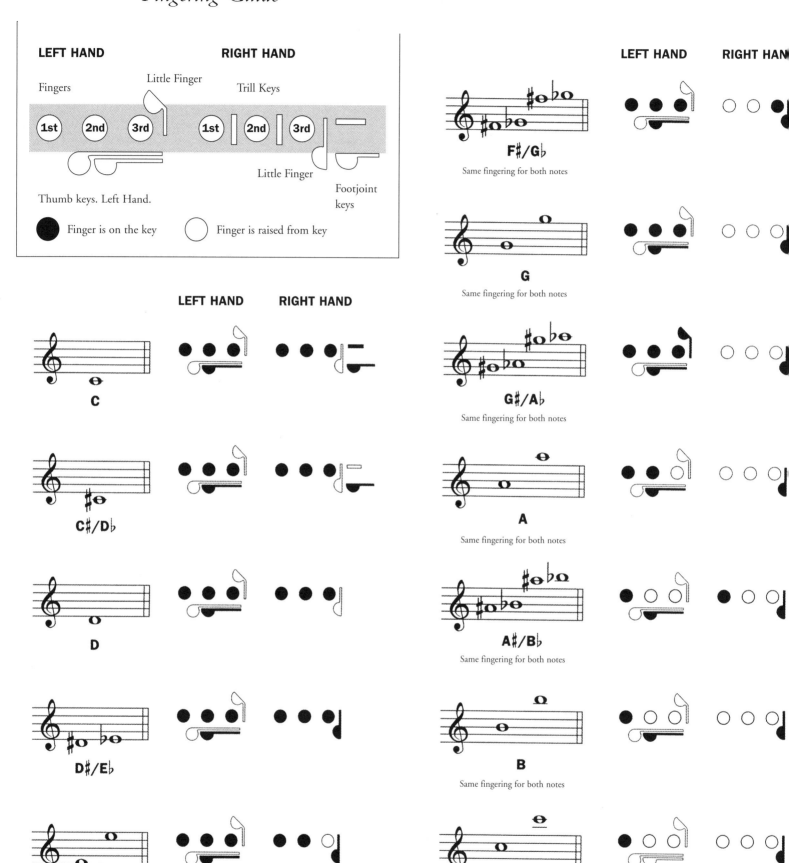

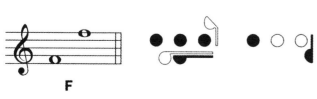

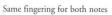

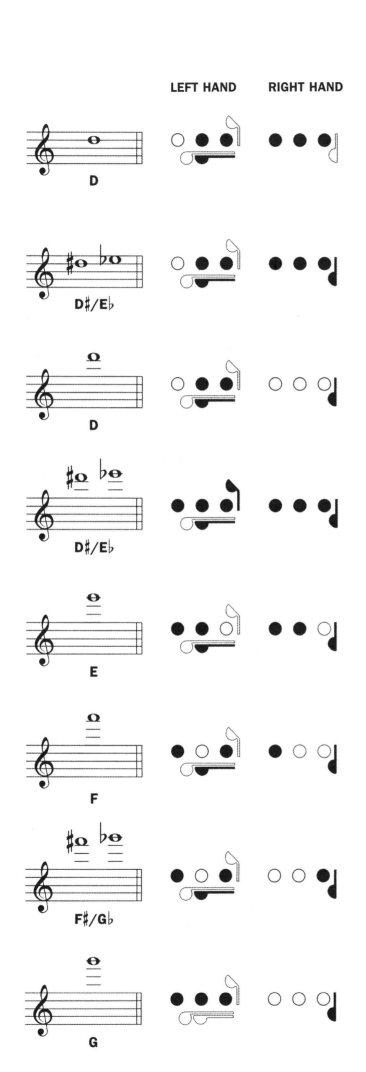

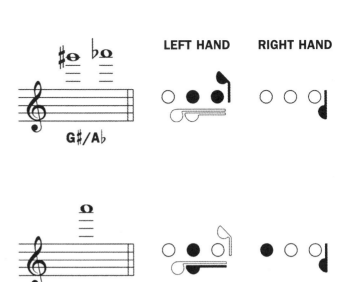

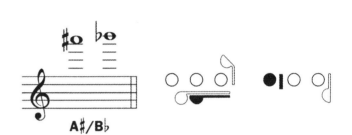

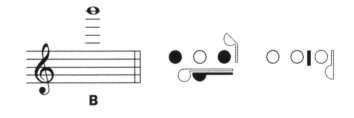

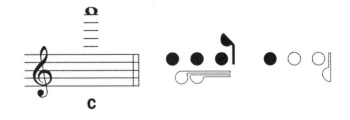

Cry Me A River

Words and Music by Arthur Hamilton

Slow (♩ = 69) 0:14

0:42

1:09

Double tempo

Guantanamera

Musical Adaptation by Pete Seeger and Julian Orbon
Lyric Adaptation by Julian Orbon, based on a poem by Jose Martí
Lyric Editor: Hector Angulo
Original Music and Lyrics by Jose Fernandez Diaz

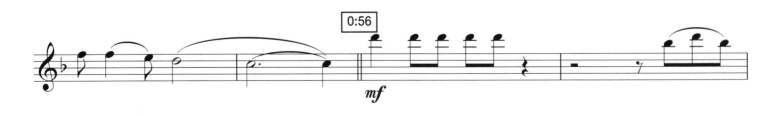

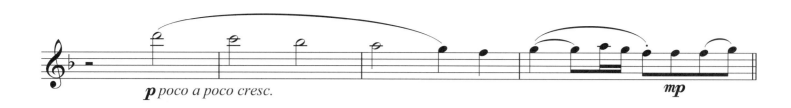

Fly Me To The Moon (In Other Words)

Words and Music by Bart Howard

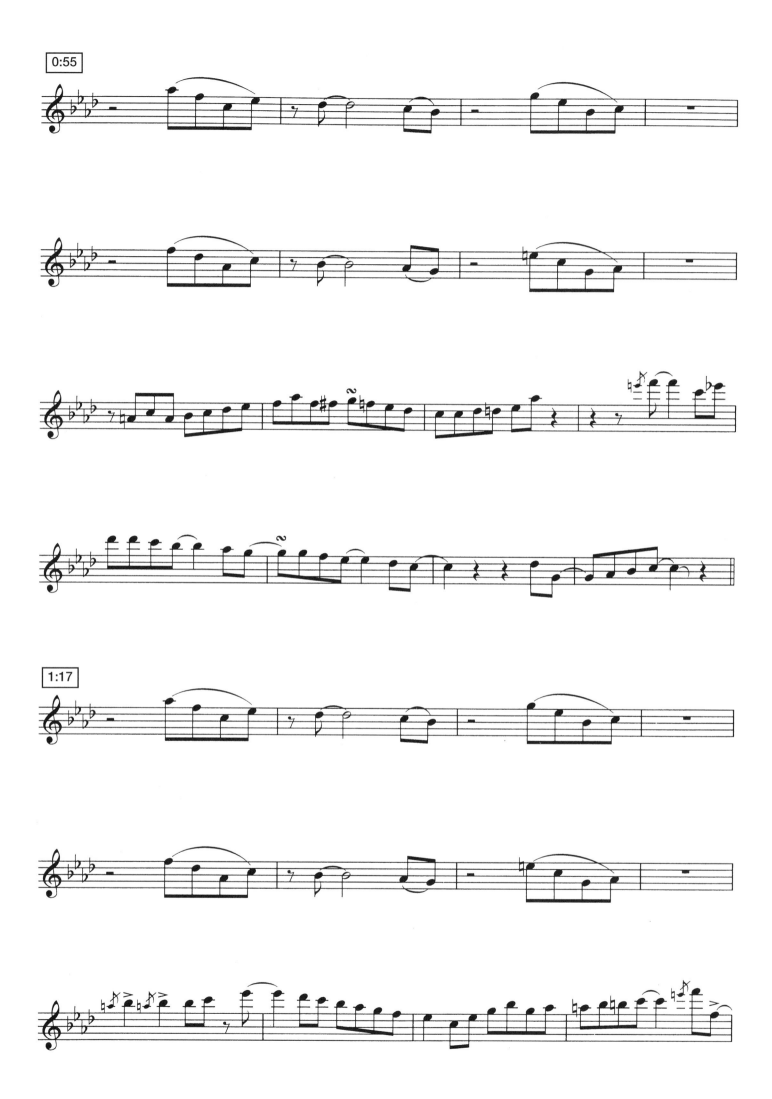

1:39

2:01 (repeat)

D.%: (with repeat) al Coda

3:01

CODA

Hit The Road Jack

Words & Music by Percy Mayfield

Medium tempo ($\quad$ = 126)

CD Track
5

I Wish I Knew How It Would Feel To Be Free

Music by Billy Taylor
Lyrics by Billy Taylor and Dick Dallas

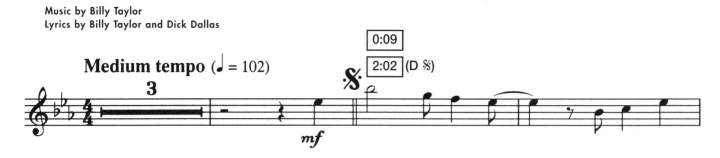

© Copyright 1964 Duane Music, Inc.
All Rights Reserved. Used by Permission.

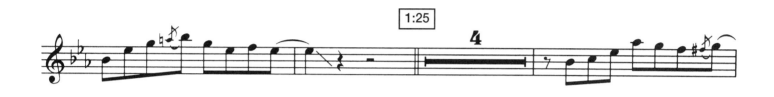

Li'l Darlin'

By Neal Hefti

Medium slow (♩ = 80) 0:12

2:36 (D 𝄉)

1:00

1:48

D. 𝄋 *al Coda*

3:12

Opus One

By Sy Oliver and Sid Garris

Perdido

By Ervin Drake, Harry Lenk and Juan Tizol

CD Track
8

Desafinado (Slightly Out Of Tune)

By Antonio Carlos Jobim and Newton Ferreira Mendonca

27

Take The "A" Train

Words and Music by Billy Strayhorn

Medium fast (♩ = 84)

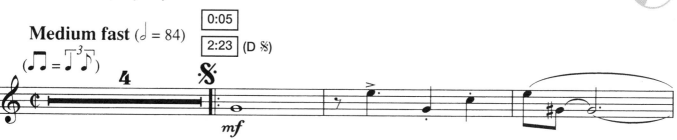

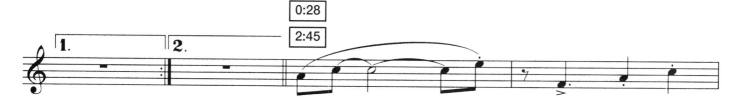

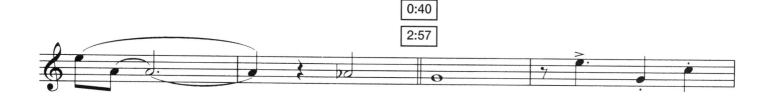

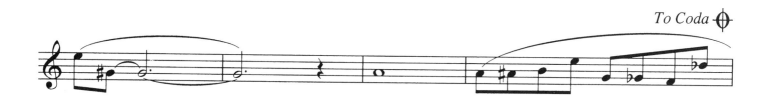

To Coda ⊕

D.𝄋 *(with repeats) al Coda*

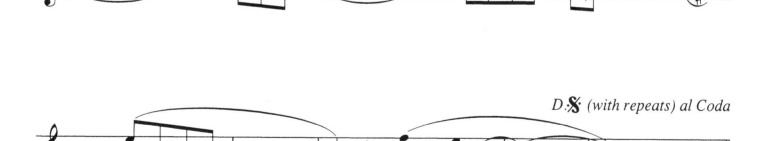

3:05

𝄌 **CODA**

Note: To help you keep your place in each song, timing markers, which correspond to the audio CD, have been included. They appear in a box at regular points in the music, e.g., 1:37

Also Available *on*

CLASSICAL GREATS
Playalong for Flute

Includes ten classical favorites with a specially record-ed backing track CD: Air (from *The Water Music*), Habañera (From *Carmen*), Jesu, Joy of Man's Desiring, Jupiter (from *The Planets Suite*), The New World Symphony (Theme), March (from *The Nutcracker Suite*), Air On The "G" String, Ode To Joy (Theme from *Symphony No. 9* "Choral"), O For The Wings Of A Dove, Spring (from *The Four Seasons*)

Order No. AM988515